The big hill

Story by Beverley Randell

Illustrations by Vaughan Duck

Little Bird

is on a big hill.

Here comes the sun.

Little Bird

is in the sun.

The big hill

is in the sun, too.

Look at Little Bird!

Look at the big hill!

The big hill

is a dinosaur.

Little Bird is up

on a **dinosaur!**

The dinosaur is hungry.

Fly, Little Bird, fly!